MAJESTIC EXPRESSIONS

Relax, Refresh, Renew

BARN QUILTS

INSPIRATIONAL ADULT COLORING BOOK

WITH ARTWORK BY
MARIAN PARSONS
OF THE BLOG
MISS MUSTARD SEED

BroadStreet
PUBLISHING

INTRODUCTION

If you've traveled through rural farmland in Sullivan County, New York, Washakie, Wyoming, Cooper, Missouri, or McCormick, South Carolina, you may have come across a barn quilt—a quilt square painted on a large piece of wood or metal (or even painted directly on the side of the barn or outbuilding). That quilt square may have been part of a series of barn quilts strung together along the countryside, creating one of the many barn quilt trails dotted around the US.

The idea of the barn quilt originated when an Ohio woman wanted to painted a quilt square and hang it on her barn as a way to honor her mother: an avid quilter. That idea blossomed into a community effort and the very first barn quilt trail in Adams County, Ohio in 2001.

Quilts have long been used to not only repurpose fabric scraps out of thrifty homemaking, but to tell stories of an individual, a family, or a community. Barn quilts have followed in that tradition. Many barn quilt squares are pulled directly from the pattern of a family quilt, but others are designed for the specific purpose of telling the story or history of the property or the family who lives there. When connected through a trail, these individual stories turn an afternoon drive through the country into a journey.

This coloring book, filled with barn quilt squares and bucolic farm scenes will bring those who color their way through it on a journey as well. A journey through original quilt squares based on traditional designs as well as squares that were inspired by encouraging Bible verses. The result is a barn quilt trail you can tour in your own home and one you get to add to with your creative coloring.

RELAX. REFRESH. RENEW.

About The Illustrator

Marian is a pastor's wife, mother of two little boys, paint and textile enthusiast, and lover of all things home. She started her business, Mustard Seed Interiors, in 2008, as a way to earn extra money for groceries. What began as a local decorative painting and mural business has grown into a popular blog (Miss Mustard Seed), an antiques and home décor business, and a paint line that is sold worldwide—Miss Mustard Seed's Milk Paint.

Marian's work has been featured in Country Living, Flea Market Style, Women's Day, Better Homes & Gardens, Fresh Style, Make It Over, Romantic Homes, Romantic Country, Farmhouse Style, Cottages & Bungalows, Fox News, NBC, CBS, and on the Nate Berkus Show. She currently lives near Gettysburg, PA, with her family and a parade of painted furniture.

Make the most
of every opportunity.
Colossians 4:5

For the Lord is good;
his steadfast love
endures forever,
and his faithfulness
to all generations.
Psalm 100:5 NRSV

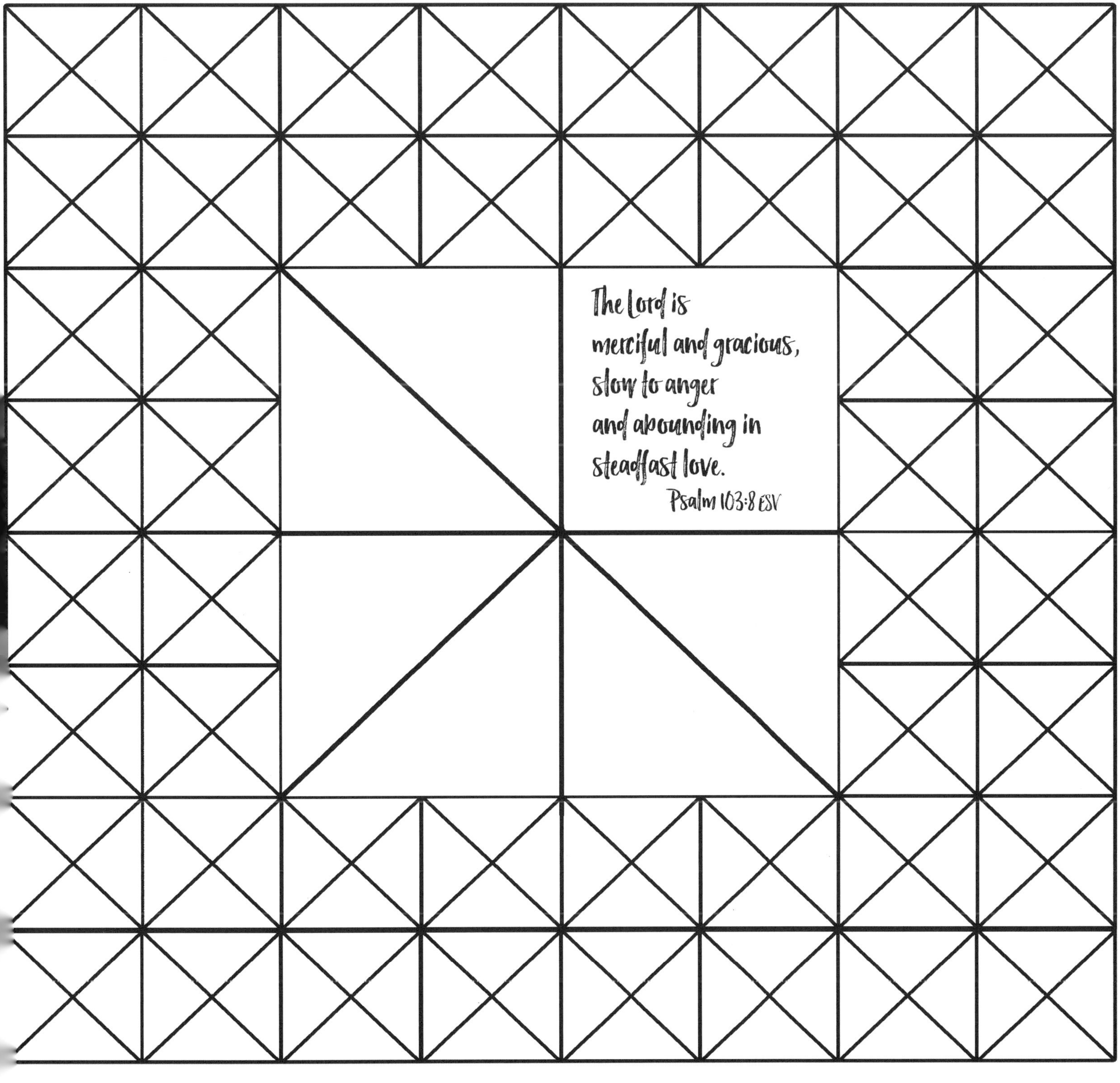
The Lord is
merciful and gracious,
slow to anger
and abounding in
steadfast love.
Psalm 103:8 ESV

"Peace I leave with you;
my peace I give you.
I do not give to you
as the world gives.
Do not let your hearts be troubled
and do not be afraid."
John 14:27

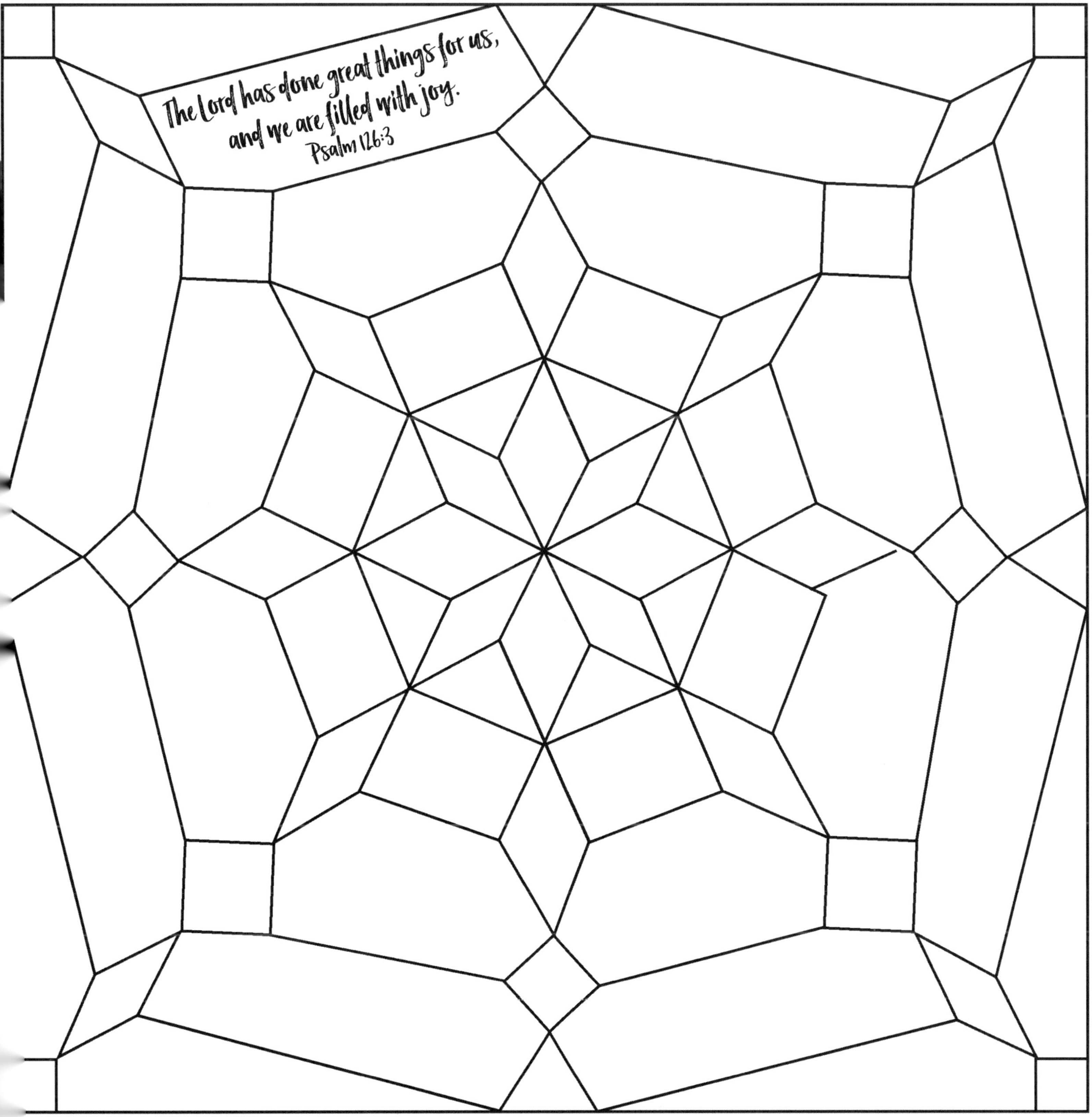
The Lord has done great things for us,
and we are filled with joy.
Psalm 126:3

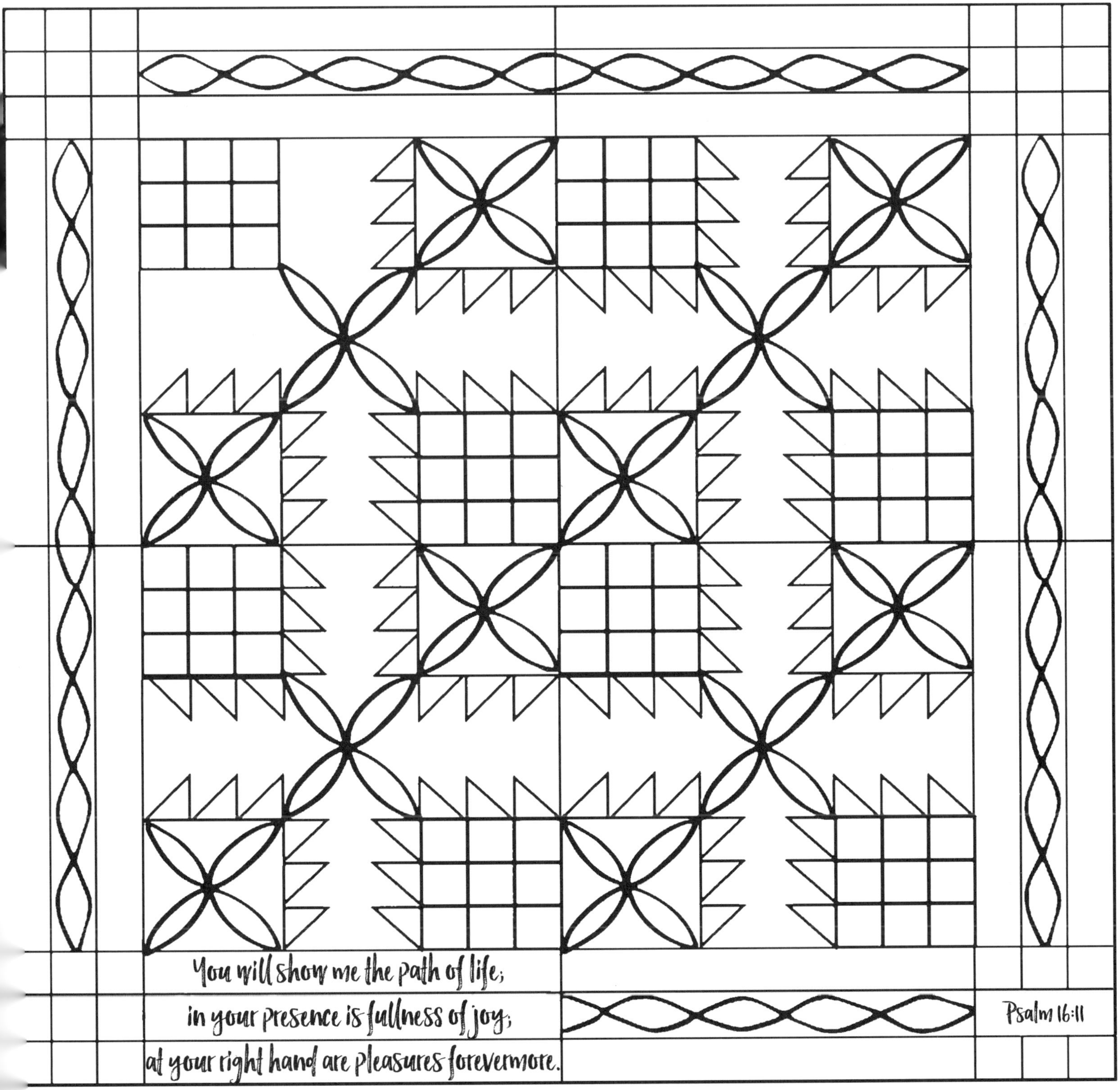
You will show me the path of life;
in your presence is fullness of joy;
at your right hand are pleasures forevermore.
Psalm 16:11

Trust in the Lord forever,
for the Lord, the Lord himself,
is the Rock eternal.
Isaiah 26:4

As for me and my household, we will serve the Lord.
Joshua 24:15

God demonstrates his own love for us in this:
While we were still sinners, Christ died for us.
Romans 5:8

The grass withers and the flowers fall,
but the word of our God endures forever.
Isaiah 40:8

"God blesses those who work for peace, for they will be called the children of God."

Matthew 5:9 NLT

The humble will see their God at work and be glad.
Let all who seek God's help be encouraged.
Psalm 69:32 NLT

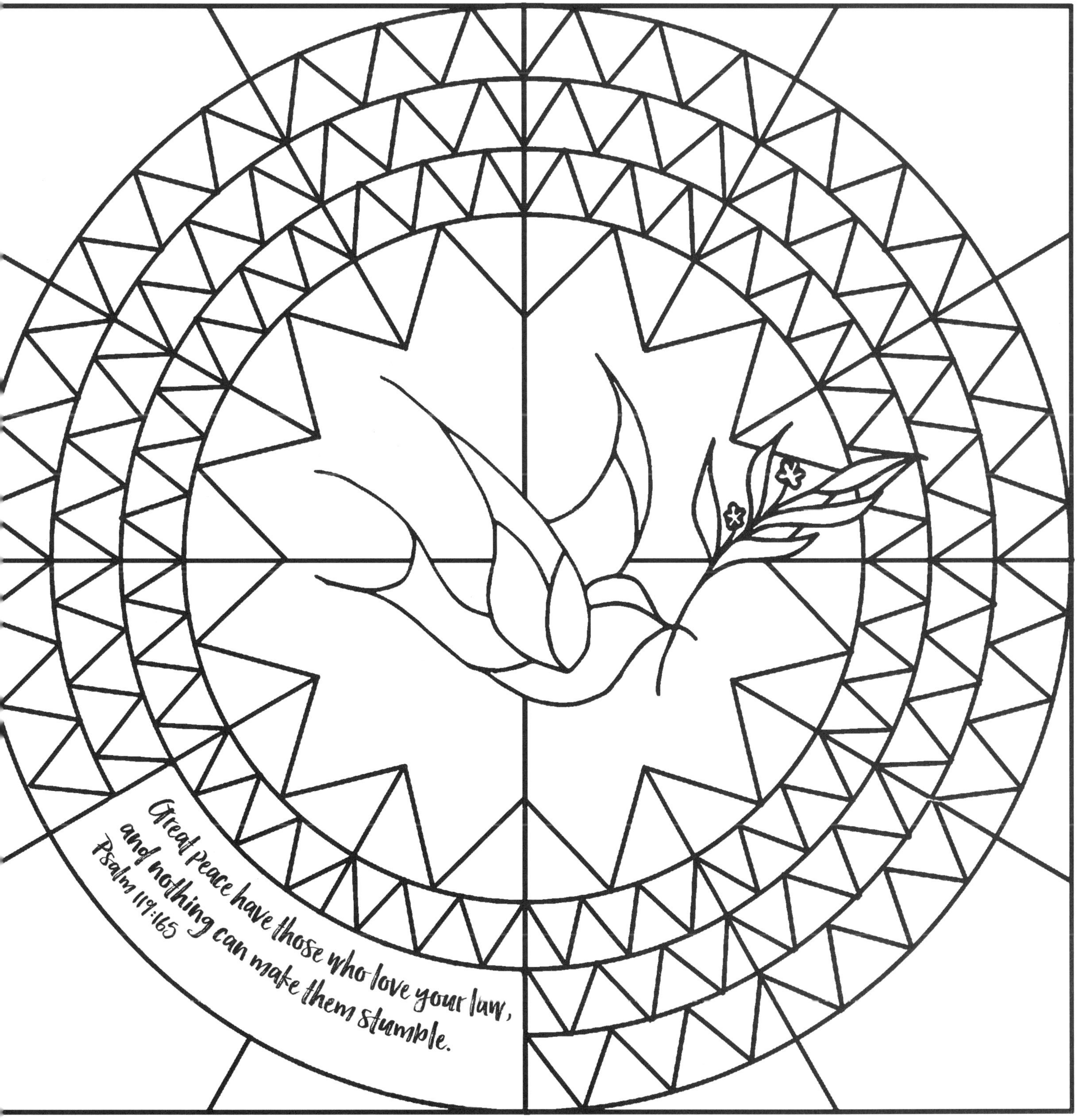
Great peace have those who love your law,
and nothing can make them stumble.
Psalm 119:165

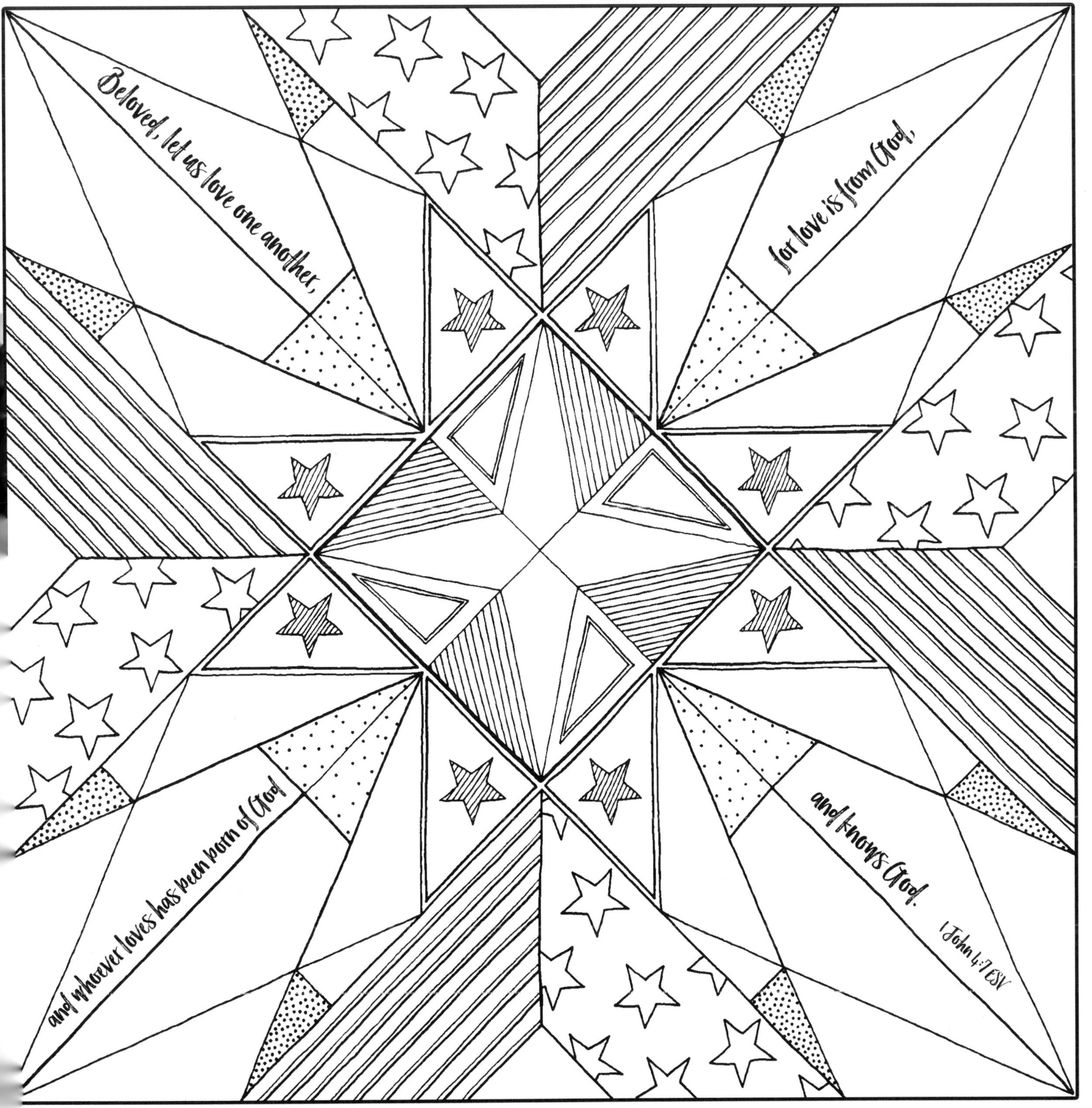
Beloved, let us love one another,
for love is from God,
and whoever loves has been born of God
and knows God.
1 John 4:7 ESV

"God so loved the world that he gave his one and only Son, that whoever believes in him shall not perish but have eternal life." John 3:16

Taste and see that the Lord is good; blessed is the one who takes refuge in him! Psalm 34:8

Before the mountains were born or you brought forth the whole world, from everlasting to everlasting, you are God. Psalm 90:2

I can do everything through Christ, who gives me strength.
Philippians 4:13 NLT

Above all else, guard your heart,
for everything you do flows from it.
Proverbs 4:23

The Lord your God will bless you in all your harvest
and in all the work of your hands, and your joy will be complete.
Deuteronomy 16:15

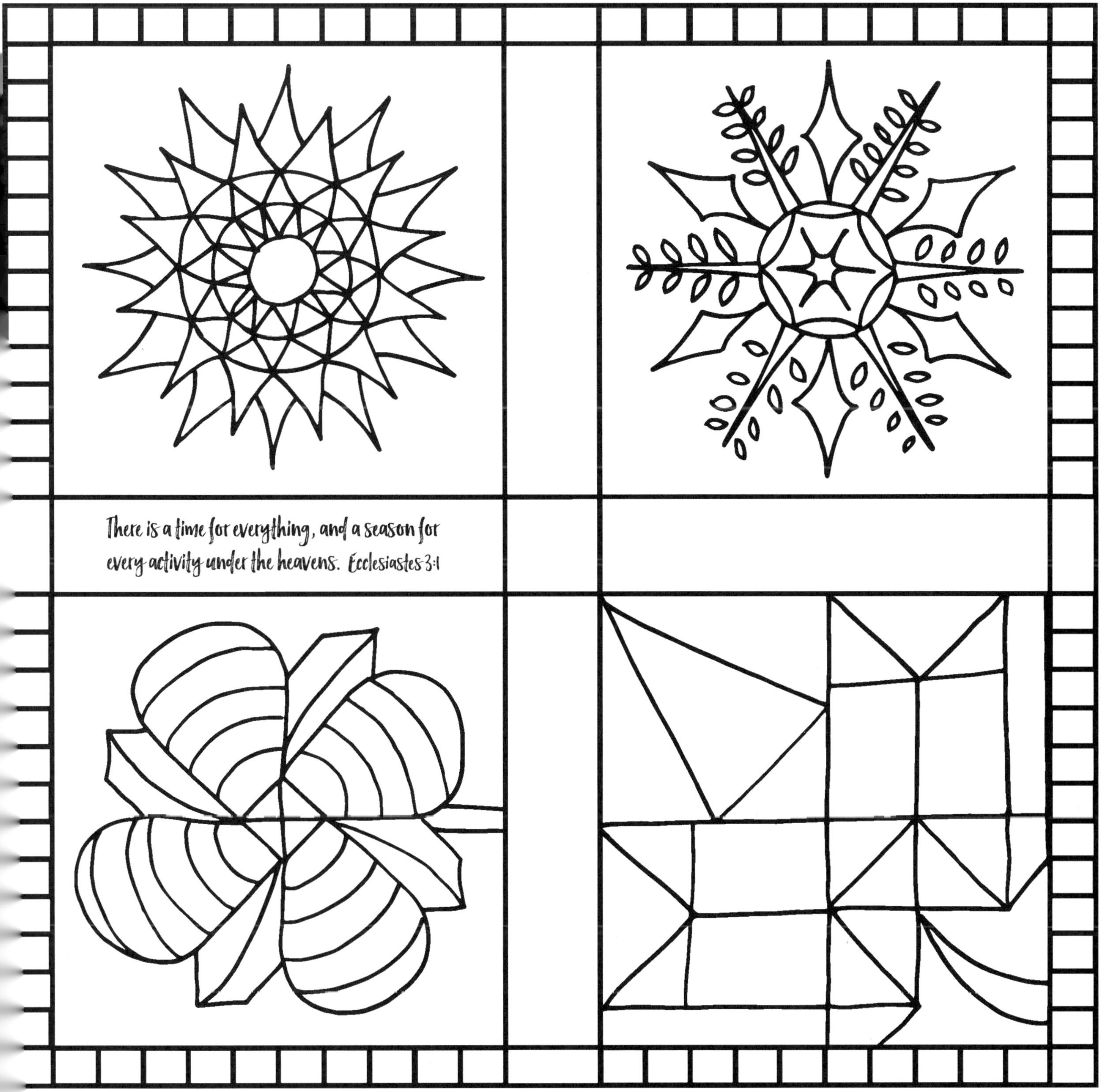
There is a time for everything, and a season for every activity under the heavens. Ecclesiastes 3:1

The Lord is my shepherd, I shall not want.
Psalm 23:1 NASB

Love does not delight in evil,
but rejoices with the truth.
It always protects, always trusts,
always hopes, always preseveres. Love never fails.

1 Corinthians 13: 6-8

I will bless the Lord at all times;
his praise shall continually be in my mouth.
Psalm 34:1 NRSV

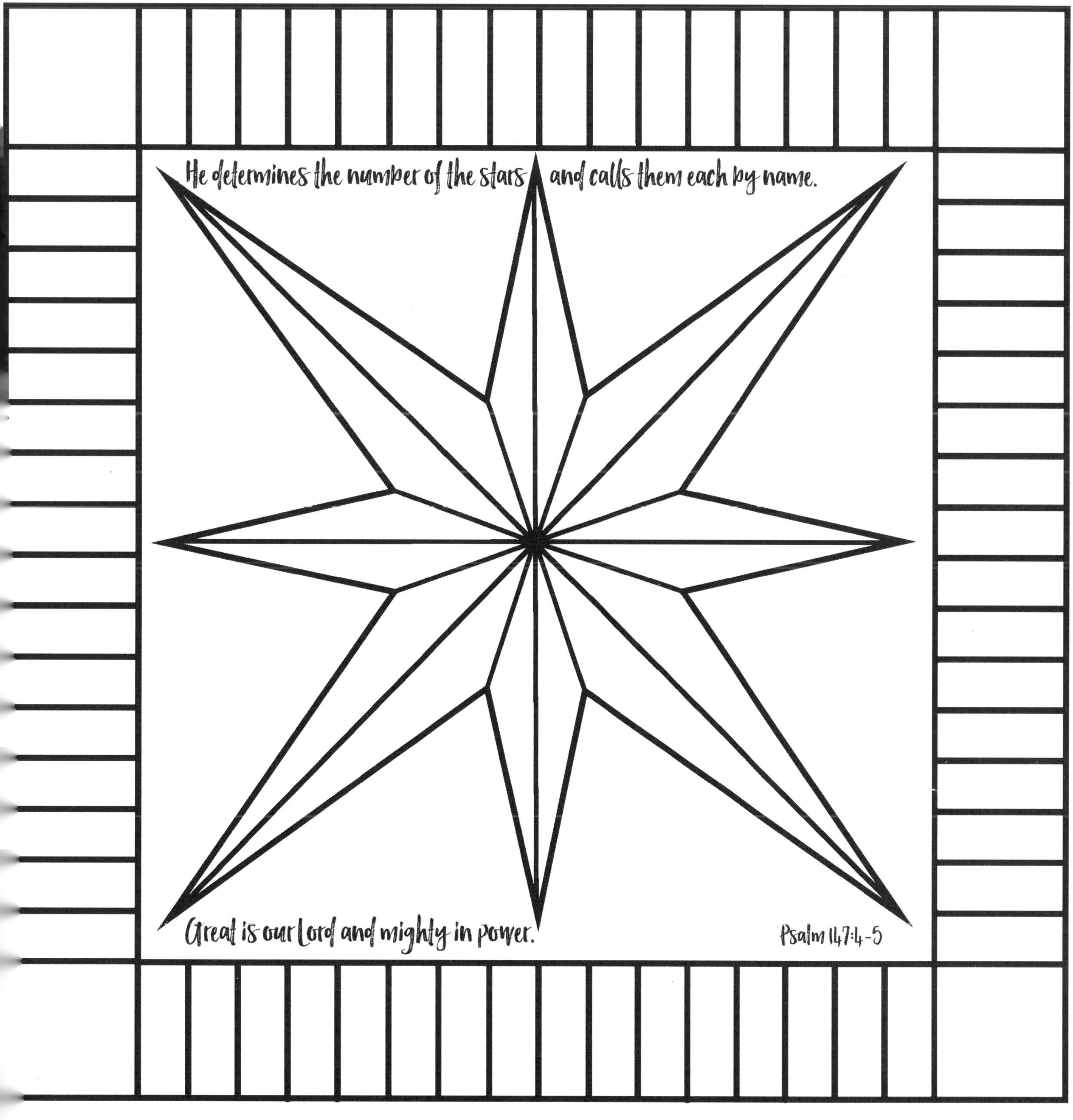
He determines the number of the stars and calls them each by name.
Great is our Lord and mighty in power.
Psalm 147:4-5

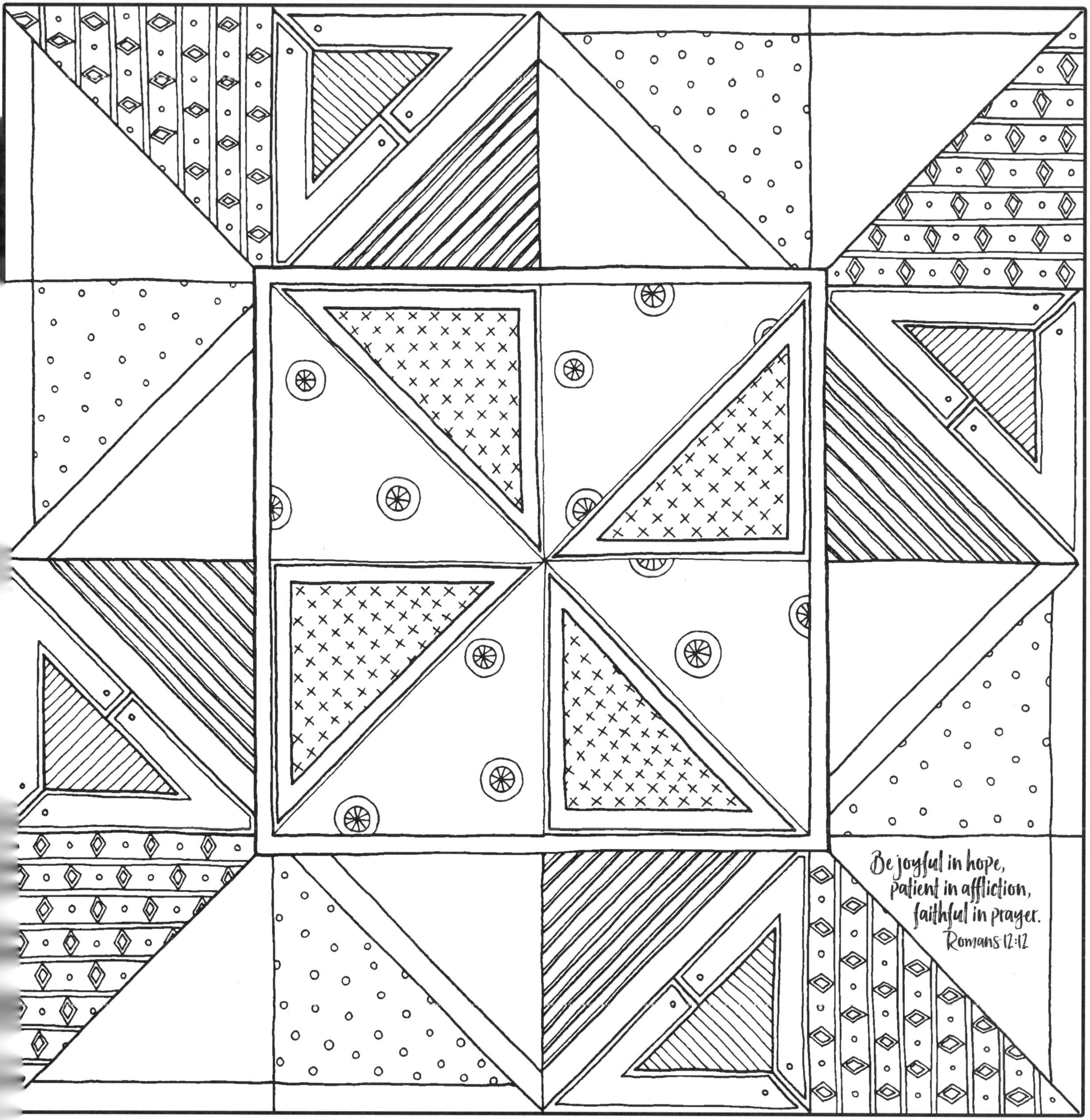
Be joyful in hope,
patient in affliction,
faithful in prayer.
Romans 12:12

And now
these three remain:
faith, hope and love.
But the greatest
of these is
love.
1 Corinthians 13:13

The Lord gives strength to his people;
the Lord blesses his people with peace.
Psalm 29:11

Delight yourself in the Lord, and he will give you the desires of your heart.

Psalm 37:4 ESV

"If you have faith as small as a mustard seed,
you can say to this mountain,
'Move from here to there,' and it will move.
Nothing will be impossible for you."

Matthew 17:20

My heart is confident
in you, O God;
my heart is confident.
No wonder I can
sing your praises!
Psalm 57:7 NLT

People who work for peace in a peaceful way
plant a good crop of right-living. James 3:18 NCV

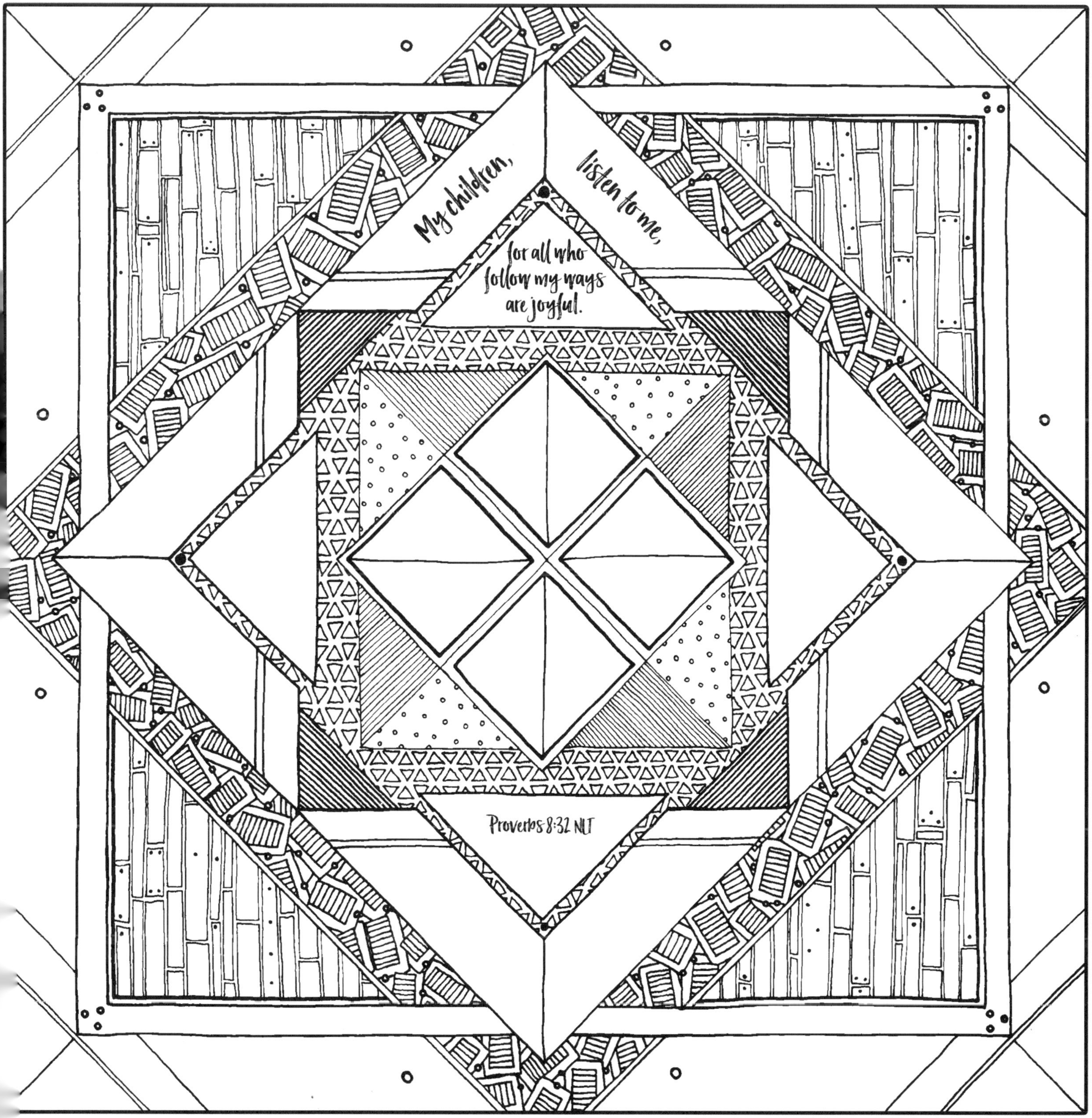
My children, listen to me,
for all who follow my ways are joyful.
Proverbs 8:32 NLT

We know the love that God has for us,
and we trust that love. God is love.
Those who live in love live in God,
and God lives in them. 1 John 4:16 NCV

See how very much
our Father loves us,
for he calls us his
children, and that is
what we are!
1 John 3:1 NLT

In the morning, Lord, you hear my voice; in the morning I lay my requests before you and wait expectantly.
Psalm 5:3

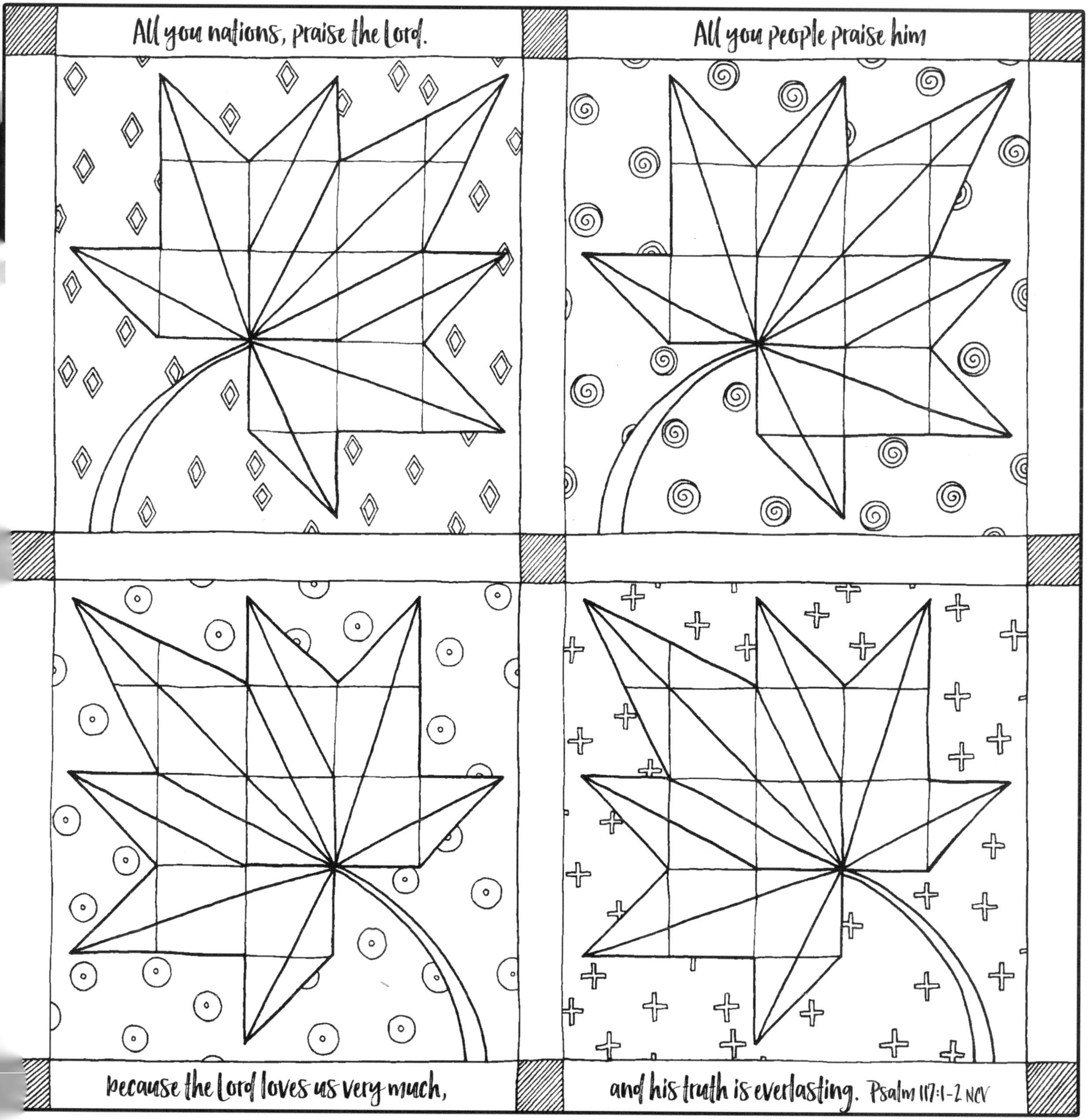
All you nations, praise the Lord.
All you people praise him
because the Lord loves us very much,
and his truth is everlasting. Psalm 117:1-2 NCV

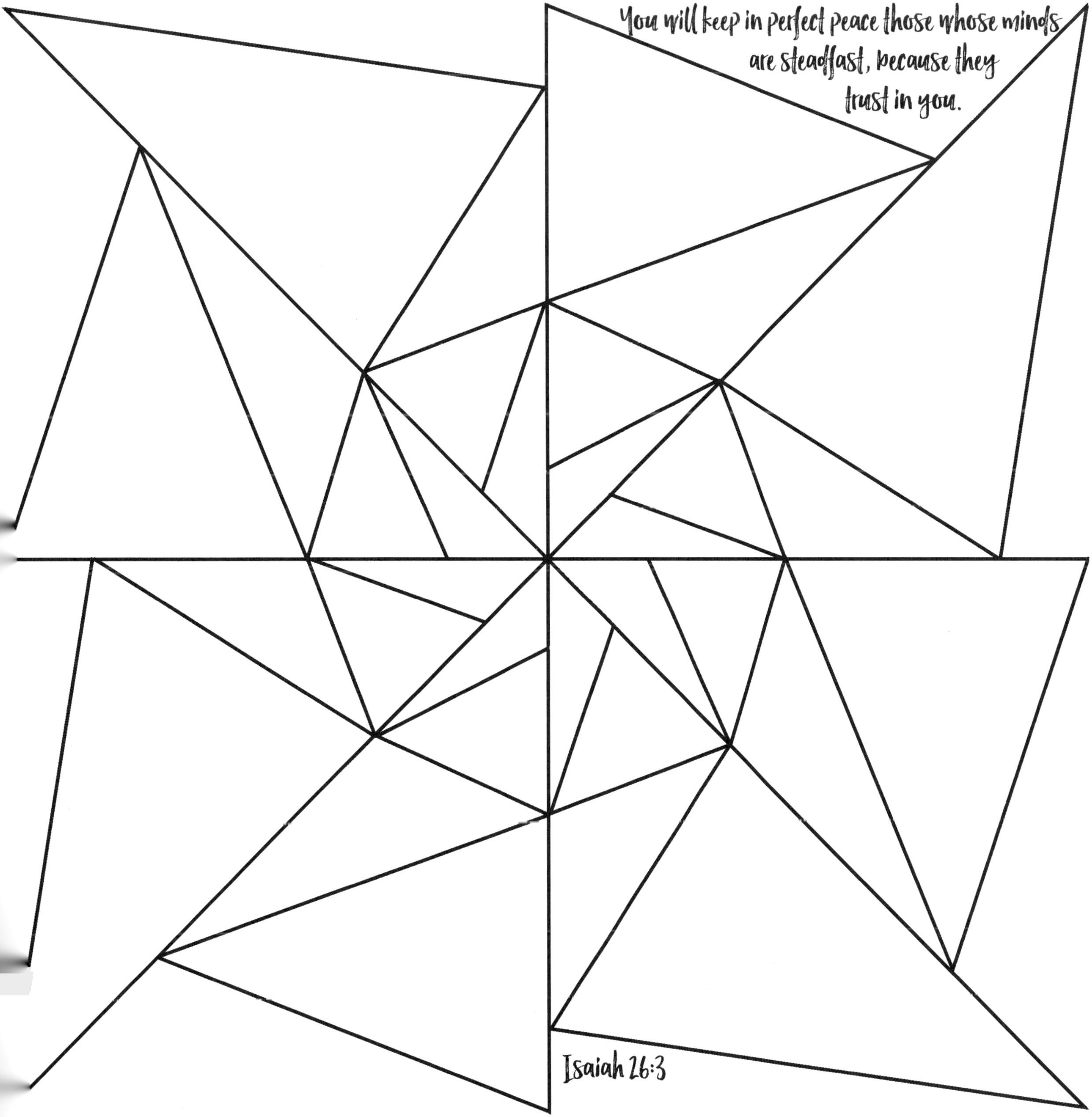

You will keep in perfect peace those whose minds are steadfast, because they trust in you.

Isaiah 26:3

"Wherever your treasure is,
there the desires
of your heart will also be."
Matthew 6:21 NLT

Be
truly glad.
There is
wonderful joy
ahead.
1 Peter 1:6 NLT

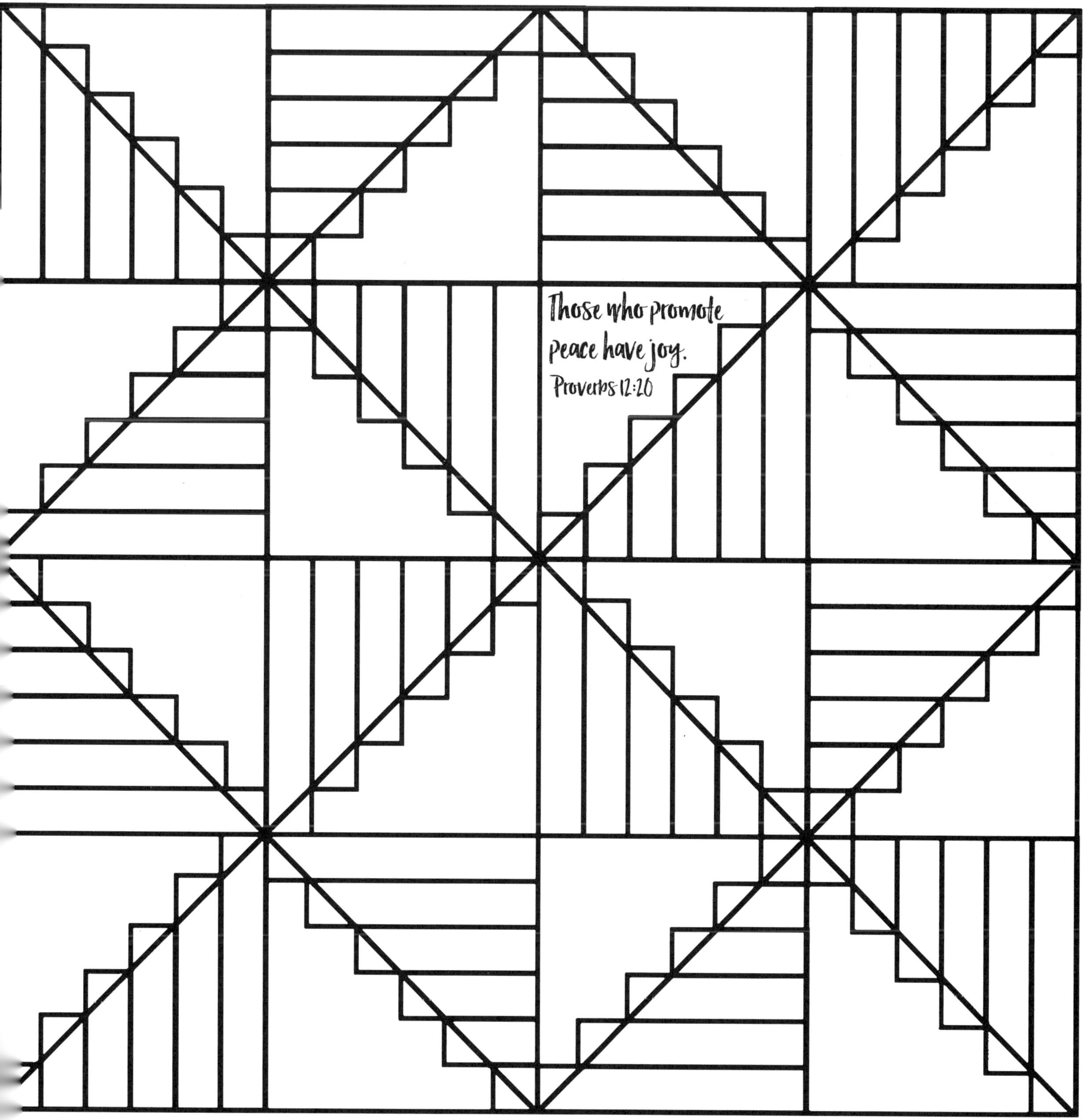
Those who promote peace have joy.
Proverbs 12:20

BroadStreet Publishing Group LLC
Racine, Wisconsin, USA
Broadstreetpublishing.com

MAJESTIC EXPRESSIONS

Barn Quilts

ISBN 978-1-4245-5397-6

Illustrations by Marian Parsons unless otherwise noted.

Cover design by Chris Garborg | garborgdesign.com
Compiled and edited by Michelle Winger | literallyprecise.com

Printed in China

17 18 19 20 21 22 23 7 6 5 4 3 2 1